EARLY AND PIONEER DIESEL & ELECTRIC LOCOMOTIVES ON BRITISH RAILWAYS

Compiled by
PETER HANDS

DEFIANT PUBLICATIONS
190 Yoxall Road
Shirley, Solihull
West Midlands

Printed on behalf of Richard Netherwood Limited, by Gorenjski tisk p.o. Slovenia.

CURRENT STEAM PHOTOGRAPH ALBUMS AVAILABLE
FROM DEFIANT PUBLICATIONS

BRITISH RAILWAYS STEAMING THROUGH THE SIXTIES

VOLUME 14
A4 size - Hardback. 96 pages
-178 b/w photographs.
£14.95 + £1.50 postage.
ISBN 0 946857 40 7.

BRITISH RAILWAYS STEAMING THROUGH THE SIXTIES

IN PREPARATION

VOLUME 15

BRITISH RAILWAYS STEAMING THROUGH THE SIXTIES

IN PREPARATION

VOLUME 16

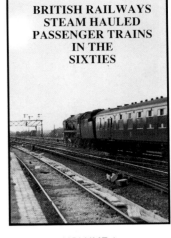

BRITISH RAILWAYS STEAM HAULED PASSENGER TRAINS IN THE SIXTIES

VOLUME 1
A4 size - Hardback. 96 pages
-177 b/w photographs.
£14.95 + £1.50 postage.
ISBN 0 946857 41 5.

BRITISH RAILWAYS STEAMING THROUGH THE FIFTIES

VOLUME 9
A4 size - Hardback. 96 pages
-177 b/w photographs.
£14.95 + £1.50 postage.
ISBN 0 946857 37 7.

BRITISH RAILWAYS STEAMING THROUGH THE FIFTIES

VOLUME 10
A4 size - Hardback. 96 pages
-176 b/w photographs.
£14.95 + £1.50 postage.
ISBN 0 946857 38 5.

BRITISH RAILWAYS STEAMING THROUGH THE FIFTIES

IN PREPARATION

VOLUME 11

BRITISH RAILWAYS STEAMING THROUGH THE FIFTIES

IN PREPARATION

VOLUME 12

BRITISH RAILWAYS STEAM HAULED PASSENGER TRAINS IN THE FIFTIES

VOLUME 1
A4 size - Hardback. 96 pages
-177 b/w photographs.
£14.95 + £1.50 postage.
ISBN 0 946857 39 3.

BRITISH RAILWAYS STEAM HAULED FREIGHT TRAINS 1948–1968

VOLUME 1
A4 size - Hardback. 96 pages
-174 b/w photographs.
£14.95 + £1.50 postage.
ISBN 0 946857 42 3.

BRITISH RAILWAYS STEAMING THROUGH THE MIDLANDS

VOLUME 1
A4 size - Hardback. 96 pages
-179 b/w photographs.
£15.95 + £1.50 postage.
ISBN 0 946857 43 I.

BRITISH RAILWAYS STEAMING ON THE EX-LNER LINES

VOLUME 3
A4 size - Hardback. 96 pages
-183 b/w photographs.
£15.95 + £1.50 postage.
ISBN 0 946857 44 X.

FUTURE STEAM PHOTOGRAPH ALBUMS
AND OTHER TITLES

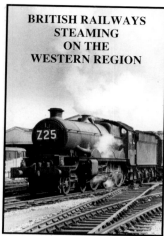

BRITISH RAILWAYS STEAMING ON THE WESTERN REGION

VOLUME 4
A4 size - Hardback. 96 pages -177 b/w photographs.
£15.95 + £1.50 postage.
ISBN 0 946857 46 6.

EARLY AND PIONEER DIESEL & ELECTRIC LOCOMOTIVES OF BRITISH RAILWAYS

A4 size - Hardback. 96 pages -177 b/w photographs.
£15.95 + £1.50 postage.
ISBN 0 946857 45 8.

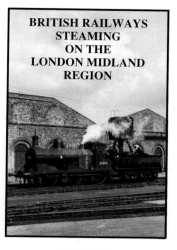

BRITISH RAILWAYS STEAMING ON THE LONDON MIDLAND REGION

VOLUME 4
A4 size - Hardback. 96 pages -177 b/w photographs.
£15.95 + £1.50 postage.
ISBN 0 946857 47 4.

BRITISH RAILWAYS STEAMING ON THE SOUTHERN REGION

IN PREPARATION

VOLUME 3

STEAM HAULED TITLED TRAINS OF BRITSH RAILWAYS

IN PREPARATION

VOLUME 1

BRITISH RAILWAYS STEAMING THROUGH CREWE, DONCASTER, EASTLEIGH AND SWINDON

IN PREPARATION

BRITISH RAILWAYS STEAMING THROUGH LONDON

IN PREPARATION

BRITISH RAILWAYS STEAMING ON THE EX-LNER LINES

IN PREPARATION

VOLUME 4

BRITISH RAILWAYS STEAM HAULED FREIGHT TRAINS 1948–1968

IN PREPARATION

VOLUME 2

BRITISH RAILWAYS STEAM HAULED PASSENGER TRAINS IN THE FIFTIES

IN PREPARATION

VOLUME 2

BRITISH RAILWAYS STEAM HAULED PASSENGER TRAINS IN THE SIXTIES

IN PREPARATION

VOLUME 2

It's a dog's life in the **FIRE SERVICE**
by Peter St.Bernard

COMEDY
269 pages. Cartoons.
£9.95 + £1.00 postage.
ISBN 0 946857 30 X.

ACKNOWLEDGEMENTS

Grateful thanks are extended to the following contributors of photographs not only for their use in this book but for their kind patience and long term loan of negatives/photographs whilst this book was being compiled.

P.BARBER TAMWORTH	W. BOYDEN BEXHILL*
B.W.L.BROOKSBANK LONDON	N. L. BROWNE ALDERSHOT
P.CANE HITCHIN	R. S. CARPENTER BIRMINGHAM
TIM FAREBROTHER BOURTON	J. M. GASCOYNE HIGH WYCOMBE
A. N. H. GLOVER BIRMINGHAM	B. K. B. GREEN WARRINGTON
R. W.HINTON GLOUCESTER	F. HORNBY NORTH CHEAM
ALAN JONES BATH	M. JOYCE HITCHIN
E. LIGHT TICKHILL	N. E. PREEDY HUCCLECOTE
G. W. SHARPE BARNSLEY	M. P. SMITH TORRINGTON
D. TITHERIDGE FAREHAM	G. H. TRURAN DUFFIELD
S. TURNBULL KIRKINTILLOCH	J. WALTON NOT KNOWN
B. WILSON SOLIHULL	J. WRAITHMELL MIRFIELD

* Courtesy of the Frank Hornby collection.

Front Cover – The last of the 'Deltic' Class Type 5 Co-Co diesel locomotives No D9021 *Argyll and Sutherland Highlander* makes the sweet 'Napier' music as it passes through Peterborough with 1E01 Edinburgh (Waverley) to London (Kings Cross) express on 2nd August 1972. All the Scottish regimental named 'Deltics' were based at Haymarket depot until their eventual transfer to York. (N.E.Preedy)

ISBN 0 946857 45 8

(C) P.B.HANDS 1994
FIRST PUBLISHED 1994

INTRODUCTION

EARLY AND PIONEER DIESEL & ELECTRIC LOCOMOTIVES OF BRITISH RAILWAYS is the first album to be released by 'Defiant Publications' which does not concentrate purely on steam locomotives, although the author has managed to sneak in the odd 'snippet' here and there within the pages of this book.

Having compiled and published in excess of forty albums from the 'BR Steaming' series, the author found it rather difficult, but challenging, to produce a book on diesel and electric traction, but without the invaluable knowledge of Norman Browne, Frank Hornby and Norman Preedy it is doubtful if 'Defiant' could have produced such an album. Every attempt has been made to provide accurate information, but if the odd mistake creeps in then it is hoped that the reader will forgive the author for his possible 'ignorance' of the subject.

As the title suggests, this album is dedicated to the early years of diesel and electric traction, from the humblest 0–4–0 shunters to the most powerful passenger and freight locomotives. Nearly all of the diesel and electric locomotives seen within the pages of this album were directly responsible for the eradication of steam from the BR system. Today, most of the earlier types of diesel and electric engines have also passed into history,

The majority of the contents of this album cover the 1950's to the early 1970's and for simplicity the chapters are divided between shunting, main line and other types in almost numerical order. The author hopes that the diesel and electric loco enthusiast will enjoy the diverse variety of locations and engine types within the pages of this album.

Apart from the 1950's and 1960's series etc., individual albums like this one will be produced from time to time. Wherever possible no famous names will be found, nor will photographs which have been published before be used, but the content and quality of photographs used will be second to none.

The 'Defiant' albums are designed to give both the ordinary everyday steam and diesel photographic enthusiast from the 1950's to the 1970's a chance to participate in and give pleasure to others whilst recapturing the days of yesteryear.

The continuation of the 'BR Steaming' series etc., depends upon *you* the reader. If you wish to join my mailing list for future albums and/or feel you have suitable photographs of steam locomotives between 1948-1968 and/or suitable photographs of early diesel/electric traction and wish to contribute them towards future albums, please contact:

Tel No.
021 745 8421

Peter Hands,
190 Yoxall Road,
Shirley, Solihull,
West Midlands B90 3RN

CONTENTS

NAMEPLATES – EXAMPLE NAMEPLATES OF BRITISH RAILWAYS DIESEL AND ELECTRIC LOCOMOTIVES.

1) English Electric Type 4 1 Co-Co 1 diesel No D216 *Campania*. (N.E.Preedy)

2) *Warship* Type 4 B-B diesel No D805 *Benbow*. (N.E.Preedy)

3) *Western* Type 4 C-C diesel No D1021 *Western Cavalier*. (Alan Jones)

4) English Electric 'Deltic' Type 5 Co-Co diesel No D9006 *The Fife and Forfar Yeomanry*. (N.E.Preedy)

5) EM1 Bo-Bo electric No 26046 *Archimedes*. (Author's Collection)

6) The 'Peak' Type 4 1 Co-Co 1 Diesel Electric locomotives (Class 45) were constructed by British Railways between 1960–1962 and all in all 127 units were built. No D32 departs from Gloucester (Eastgate) under clear signals in some very wintry conditions on 9th December 1967. D32 is in charge of 1N 70, a Bristol (Temple Meads) to Newcastle (Central) express. Note the steam style shedplate which is affixed beneath the train reporting number. (N.E.Preedy)

7) No D100 *Sherwood Forester* was commissioned on 13th May 1961 and allocated to 17A Derby. Although it acquired its nameplates at Derby Works on 18th September 1961 it was 'officially' named at Derby station five days later. It is seen at the Basingstoke Rail Exhibition on 26th September 1987 (preserved) after having its nameplates restored. *Sherwood Forester* is a credit to its owners as it gleams in the sun after the renaming ceremony. (N.E.Preedy)

8) No D46 stands between two breakdown cranes and a pile of debris after a freight train derailment at Ashchurch on 4th May 1968. Front end damage to D46 is evident, but as these hefty locomotives turned the scales at over 138 tons it is not surprising that the wagons came off worst. Constructed by October 1961, D46 was initially based at 14A Cricklewood. It was renumbered 45037 in January 1975 and taken out of service in July 1988. (N.E.Preedy)

9) One of the original 'Peaks' (Class 44) No D4 *Great Gable* began its working life on 26th September 1959 on the West Coast Main Line at 1B Camden. On 7th July 1971 *Great Gable*, in rather unkempt external condition, passes through Toton yard with a rake of coal wagons. Renumbered 44004 in April 1974 it was withdrawn in November 1980. In June 1981 it was sold to the Midland Railway Trust at Butterley and has been a 'star' at many open days. (N.E.Preedy)

10) Different styles of English Electric diesel locomotives meet at Euston station on 25th March 1961 after arriving with up expresses. On the right is 'Peak' Class (44) No D2 *Helvellyn* (1B Camden) whilst on the left is 'D200' Class (40) No D225 (named *Lusitania* on 28th March 1962 at Crewe Works). *Helvellyn* was withdrawn from Toton shed in February 1979 with *Lusitania* following suit from Longsight (Manchester) in October 1982. (F.Hornby)

11) It has been many years since the West Coast Main Line was unfettered by overhead electric wires and pylons, but on 5th May 1962 electrification of this section was still a number of years away. English Electric Type 4 diesel (Class 40) No D310 speeds through South Kenton with the northbound *Mid-day Scot* consisting of ten coaches. The tracks at either side of the island platform have third rail D.C. current for the local electric trains. (N.L.Browne)

12) On the same day the photographer has swivelled round and his camera has been pointed in the opposite direction at South Kenton. No D297 (1B Camden) on an eight coach up express passes a Bakerloo Line underground train which is travelling on the former LMS D.C. line to Watford. Coming into service at 5A Crewe (North) in October 1960, D297 was renumbered 40097 in March 1974. It was condemned in June 1983 after derailment damage. (N.L.Browne)

13) Only days before the demise of steam on British Railways No D347 is photographed from the top of a condemned steam locomotive in the yard at 9D Newton Heath on 27th July 1968. D347 is passing the signalbox of the same name with an eastbound tanker train. The coaling plant in the left of this picture was later demolished and the depot converted for diesel traction. D347 (40147) survived until September 1980 – cut up in August 1983. (J.M.Gascoyne)

14) Like all of the early diesels No D245, built by November 1959 and shedded at 52A Gateshead, was painted in green livery. On 30th July 1967 it is in an ex.works condition with the all-over BR livery at Bradford (Exchange). The pristine condition of D245 is in stark contrast to LMS Class 5 4–6–0 No 44896, from 55A Leeds (Holbeck) . Note the Mini car in the foreground, the design and production of which is still with us today, unlike 44896 and D245. (N.E.Preedy)

15) The 'D200' Type 4 diesels, of which 200 were built, were constructed between 1958–1962 at the Vulcan Foundry and by Robert Stephenson & Hawthorns at Darlington. The pioneer engine, D200 is photographed at 30A Stratford in March 1958. The first batch of these locomotives served on former Great Eastern Railway metals and eventually helped to oust the BR *Britannia* Pacifics from the same. Today, D200 (40122) is actively preserved. (N.E.Preedy)

16) We take our leave of the 2000 horse-power 'D200' Class diesels with this smartly turned out example, No D262, from 64B Haymarket, as it basks in sunshine outside 52B Heaton (Newcastle) on 4th September 1960. Then only six months old it gave over twenty-one years of service before withdrawal from Carlisle (Kingmoor) in November 1981 as No 40062. Stored at Kingmoor and Swindon Works it was cut up at the latter in June 1983. (N.L.Browne)

17) By the time the Class 50 Co-Co Diesel Electric 'D400' Class locomotives were introduced into service at the end of 1967 steam was in its death throes. Nevertheless they were seen by many to put the final nail in the coffin for steam in Britain. On 10th September 1971 a trio of these Type 4's are lined up at Polmadie depot in Glasgow, Nos 441, 425 and 432. In their early days they worked on the West Coast Main Line north from Crewe. (N.E.Preedy)

18) All 50 units of Class 50 were built at the Vulcan Foundry, Newton-le-Willows with Engish Electric being the main contractor and for many years they were hired to rather than owned by British Railways. On 5th May 1968 No D423 has just arrived at Crewe from Newton-le-Willows for acceptance trials. At this time the loco was not fitted with multiple opration jumper cables. D423 was one of the first members to be renumbered, 50023 in December 1973. (N.E.Preedy)

19) D444 at Crewe having just handed over express 1M27 to electric traction on 1st June 1971. Introduced into main line service on 12th October 1968, D444 was renumbered 50044 in February 1974 three months before being transferred to Bristol Bath Road depot. It was named *Exeter* at Exeter St.Davids station on 27th April 1978 with crests applicable to the same being unveiled at the aforementioned location on 20th August 1981. (N.E.Preedy)

20) In company with several of her sisters, No D440 rests at Crewe North depot on 30th March 1969 some six months after construction. This powerful locomotive (2750 hp.), weighing some 117 tons, continued to work with the other members of the class on the Crewe to Glasgow route until the coming of full electrification when they were drafted to the Western region to replace the '*Western*' diesels. Named *Leviathan* in September 1978. (F.Hornby)

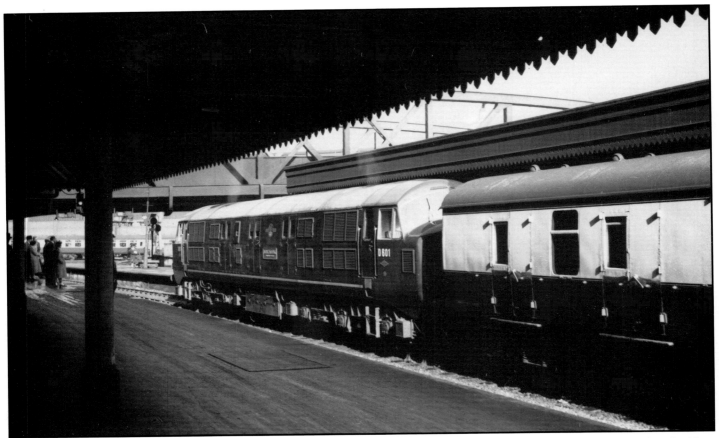

21) Once the Western Region authorities were convinced of the superiority of diesel-hydraulic traction an order was placed with the North British Locomotive Company in Glasgow for five Type 4 A1A–A1A locomotives powered by 2000 hp M.A.N. engines. Constructed in 1958/59 they received famous warship names and the legend of the *Warship* Class was born. No D601 *Ark Royal* heads the down *Cornish Riviera* express at Paddington in October 1958. (G.H.Truran)

22) The famous N.B.L. Co. diamond-shaped works plate is clearly visible on the cab side of Warship Class No D602 *Bulldog* on shed at 82C Swindon on 20th September 1959. Originally it was planned to extend the class to Nos. D605–D637, but regrettably the North British Company's venture into diesel traction was far from trouble-free and the five members built only had an active life of nine years being withdrawn in December 1967. (N.E.Preedy)

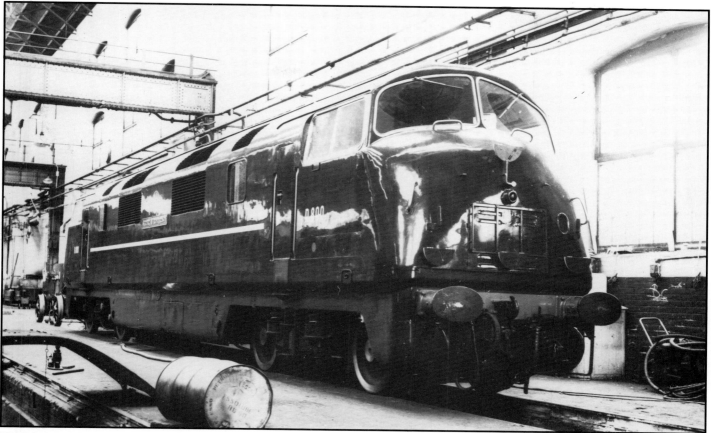

23) Of the 'D800' Class B–B Diesel Hydraulics, Nos D800–D832 & D866–D870 were built at Swindon Works, with Nos D833–D865 being constructed by the North British Railway Company. The pioneer locomotive No D800 *Sir Brian Robertson* was named after the then Chairman of the British Transport Commission. D800 is seen inside the 'A' Shop at Swindon Works on 27th July 1958 a few days after being officially named at Paddington station. (N.E.Preedy)

24) The 'D800' series of Type 4 Diesel Hydraulics was rather more successful than the heavier, but less powerful 'D600 ' version. Weighing between 78 and 80 tons they were appreciably lighter than their diesel-electric contemporaries and with the exception of D800 they were also named after warships. On 4th April 1959 No D801 *Vanguard* hurries the down *Royal Duchy*, from Paddington to Penzance, past the locomotive shed at 81C Southall. (F.Hornby)

25) A massive construction job dominates the skyline in the background of this picture taken at Bristol (Temple Meads) on 12th July 1969. In the foreground in truly 'magnificent' external condition is Swindon built *Warship* No 828 *Magnificent*, from 84A Laira (Plymouth). *Magnificent's* revenue earning days were brought to a slightly premature end after it caught fire near Yatton on 2nd July 1971 whilst heading a train of ammonia tanks. (N.E.Preedy)

26) North British built *Warship* No D839 *Relentless*, of 83A Newton Abbot, reaches the end of its journey from Paddington and sweeps round the sharp curve on the approach to Bristol (Temple Meads) with the down *Bristolian* in the summer of 1962. In previous years this service had been the preserve of GWR *Castle* Class 4–6–0's. Constructed in November 1960, *Relentless* only had a working life of eleven years and was cut up at Swindon Works. (N.E.Preedy)

27) Two diesel hydraulic locomotives built by outside contractors grace the railway scene at Swindon Works on 21st May 1961. Nearest the camera is a North British Locomotive Company product *Warship* Class B–B No D838 *Rapid* (built by October 1960). Behind *Rapid* is the pioneer member of the 'Hymeck' Class B–B's No D7000 having not long been delivered from the Beyer Peacock Works at Gorton in Manchester. (N.L.Browne)

28) Steam and diesel traction share the limelight at Exeter St.Davids station in August 1960. In the left of the frame is SR Unrebuilt *Battle of Britain* Class 4–6–2 No 34061 *73 Squadron*, from 72A Exmouth Junction, which is ignored by the railwaymen on the right hand platform who are distracted by the presence of an almost brand new *Warship* No D822 *Hercules*. The latter was to die after only eleven years whereas the former had a life of seventeen years. (B.Wilson)

29) A class which was destined to become extremely popular with enthusiasts, the 2700hp *Western* C–C Type 4 Diesel Hydraulics (later Class 52), first appeared in service in December 1961 . On 25th July 1974 No D1037 *Western Empress* (built at Crewe Works in August 1962) emerges from Parsons Tunnel at Teignmouth with the 10.30am from Paddington to Paignton. The sea wall section of line was a fine location to see and photograph these handsome machines. (N.E.Preedy)

30) Although the bulk of the seventy-four members of the *Western* class did not appear until some fourteen years after nationalisation there were still echoes of the old GWR in the cast numberplates and repetitive names – all prefixed "Western". In this photograph No D1008 *Western Harrier* is almost brand new at Paddington station after bringing an up express into this mighty terminus on 22nd September 1962. (F.Hornby)

31) The prototype member of the "Western" Class was first seen by the author under construction at Swindon Works on 28th May 1961 and it was not realised at the time that these diesels were to sound the death knell for the GWR *King* Class 4–6–0's. On 6th September 1964 the *Kings* were but a memory as No D1000 *Western Enterprise* stands at Swindon Works in company with a *Warship*. D1000 is painted in the experimental 'desert sand' livery. (N.E.Preedy)

32) Swindon built *Western* Class No D1006 *Western Stalwart*, from 82A Bristol (Bath Road), stands light engine by a signal gantry at Gloucester on 28th November 1965. The locomotive has a marine type windscreen wiper which was fitted as an experiment, but not adopted as standard. Released into traffic in June 1962 *Western Stalwart* was taken out of service in April 1975, but it languished at Swindon Works for two years before being cut up. (N.E. Preedy)

33) Remaining at Gloucester we espy No D1007 *Western Talisman* (84A Laira – Plymouth) leaving the long closed Eastgate station with the lunchtime Cheltenham to Paddington express on 22nd May 1969. The site of this once important station now forms part of the inner ring road. *Western Talisman* suffered severe damage in an accident at Ealing on 19th December 1973 and was condemned the following month. It was scrapped at Swindon a year later. (N.E.Preedy)

34) The production of the "Western" Class Diesel Hydraulics was shared between Crewe and Swindon Works. One of the Crewe built batch, No D1065 *Western Consort*, another Laira based engine, is noted fresh from overhaul outside Swindon Works on 3rd May 1964. *Western Consort* is in the attractive maroon livery which became the standard colour of the class until the arrival of the BR blue livery. D1065 survived in service until November 1976. (N.E.Preedy)

35) We take our leave of the "Western" diesel hydraulics with this fine portrait of No D1003 *Western Pioneer* which is heading the *Cornish Riviera* express, curiously with an ex. LNER carriage next to the locomotive, at Exeter St.Davids in July 1962. These fine machines seemed to fit in so well in Devon and Cornwall where they put in so much of their finest work. The class was rendered extinct in February 1977. Nos D1010/13/15/23/41/48/62 are preserved. (G.H.Truran)

36) Numerically the largest and undoubtedly the most successful of BR's Type 4 fleet are the diesel electric Brush 'D1500' Class Co-Co's, now universally known as the Class 47's. On a sun-drenched 4th July 1973 No D1696, of Bescot shed, drifts through Sonning Cutting, east of Reading, with an engineers train. This 'birds-eye' view location was much favoured by photographers of steam locomotives during the fifties and sixties. (N.E.Preedy)

37) Apart from being successful the 'D1500's were also very versatile and they eventually numbered 512 strong. Crewe Works/Brush built (May 1965) No D1843 (DO5 Stoke on Trent Division) breaks the monotony of 'electric multiple units' at Guildford station on 1st August 1970. D1843 is in charge of a through express to the Western Region. Note that this locomotive (renumbered 47193 in April 1974) is still in two-tone green livery. (F.Hornby)

38) The first batch of 'D1500' locomotives were allocated to 34G Finsbury Park Diesel Depot and for years worked side by side with the 'Deltics' on expresses on the East Coast Main Line. No 1506 passes a motionless diesel multiple unit in a siding as it arrives at Grantham on 8th September 1973 with 1DO2, the 12.20pm express from Kings Cross to Cleethorpes. Becoming No 47407 in February 1974 it was named *Aycliffe* in November 1984. (N.E.Preedy)

39) The bulk of the Brush Type 4 (Class 47) locomotives were numbered D1500–D1999 and so to accommodate the final twelve members (built 1966/67) they were numbered D1100–D1111 . The last but one example, No 1110, is overshadowed by the signalbox at Kings Cross station on 17th July 1971 whilst performing manouvres in the depot yard. No 1110 is in the two-tone green livery as built, which seemed to suit these engines very well. (N.E.Preedy)

40) On a visit to Crewe Works on 7th February 1965 with a society special from Birmingham (New Street), hauled by BR *Britannia* Class 4–6–2 No 70042 *Lord Roberts*, the author noted Brush Type 4's Nos D1658–Dl681 under various stages of construction. All were destined for depots on the Western Region and the bulk of these were the only examples of the class to be named for a long time. One of them, No 1673 *Cyclops* is at Gloucester depot on 19th September 1969 (N.E.Preedy)

41) Looking at this photograph taken at Crewe station on 1st April 1967, with the overhead electric wires and presence of main line diesels, it is amazing to record that steam was still being used at Crewe at this stage in time on expresses to and from Carlisle. In this picture, however, there is not a 'steamer' in sight. The scene is dominated by two Brush Type 4's Nos D1848 (two-tone green) and D1957 (BR 'rail blue'). (D.Titheridge)

42) A fine panoramic view of the railway scene at Gloucester in February 1969 with a splendid selection of upper and lower quadrant signals on view. Points and trackwork are covered in snow after a blizzard as is the front end of Brush Type 4 No 1957 as it accelerates a Cardiff to Newcastle express out of the station. From around December 1973 to March 1979 this engine was renumbered three times. It was named *Lothian* in April 1979. (N.E.Preedy)

43) For the time being we move away from the 'glamorous' main line diesels to the world of small and not so small diesel shunters which were the work-horses behind the scenes at many locations. BR built 0–6–0 204hp shunter No 2164 is seen in blue livery at Stratford Depot in East London on 24th February 1973. After withdrawal in January 1976 as No 03164 it eventually found its way to Italy, being seen as late as 1984 in Trieste. (N.E.Preedy)

44) As can be clearly seen in both this photograph and the one above, some diesel shunters had 'funnels' not too dissimilar to steam locomotives and all had coupling rods. Two Class 03 0–6–0 204hp diesel shunters stand outside their birthplace at Swindon Works on 28th May 1961. The nearest to the camera, No D2194 is brand new, whilst No D2146 had been constructed three months earlier. They were both withdrawn in September 1968. (N.L.Browne)

45) Drewry 04 Class 0–6–0 Diesel Shunter No D2202 at 31B March shed on 10th April 1960. This engine commenced its working life as No 11102 in June 1952 and was renumbered D2202 in January 1958. Equipped with a Gardner 8L3 204hp Diesel Mechanical engine No D2202 was fitted with cow-catchers and side protection for work on the Wisbech & Upwell Tramway. Withdrawn from Crewe Works in February 1968 it was scrapped at Cohens, Kettering. (N.L. Browne)

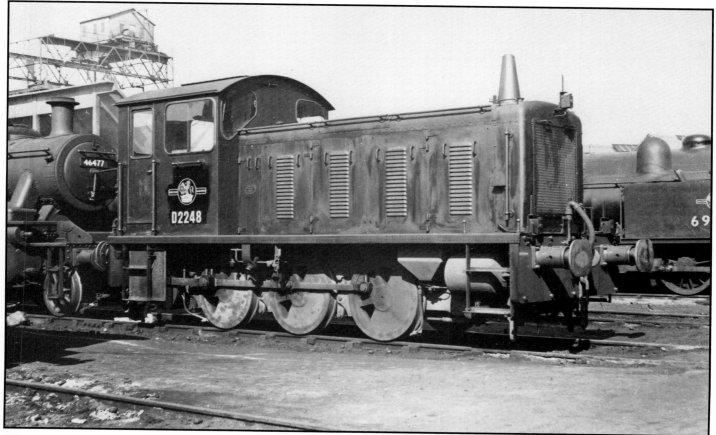

46) Drewry 0–6–0 Diesel Mechanical Shunter (Class 04) No D2248 is seen at its home depot of 51A Darlington in 1961 surrounded by steam locomotives including LMS Class 2 2–6–0 No 46477. Quite a number of these diesels were to be found at depots in the North East and took some tracking down. D2248 (11218) was sold to the National Coal Board after withdrawal in June 1970, firstly at Manvers Main and then at Maltby Main Colliery. (N.E.Preedy)

47) Hunslet 204hp 0–6–0 Diesel Mechanical Shunter (later Class 05) No 11140, renumbered D2554 in January 1959, poses for the camera at Parkeston shed on 25th May 1956. In the background is LNER J39 Class 0–6–0 No 64787 as the little shunter goes about its business. D2554 changed numbers again in August 1974 to 05001 and to 97803 (Departmental Stock) in January 1981. Drafted to the Isle of Wight in June 1966 it is preserved there today. (N.E.Preedy)

48) The series of 0–4–0 Diesel Shunters Nos D2410–D2444 were constructed by Andrew Barclay & Sons, Kilmarnock between 1958 and 1960. All were allocated to sheds on the Scottish Region. On 23rd June 1959 No D2415 (61A Keith) stands alone at Keith Junction station. Of the original thirty-five units only ten survived to be renumbered as Class 06 locomotives. D2415 was not one of them, being condemned from 64H Leith Central in June 1968. (A.N.H. Glover)

49) At its height the lengthy straight running shed at 64A St.Margarets (Edinburgh) was packed with steam locomotives, from mighty Pacifics to the humblest of tank engines, but by 11th July 1967 it was a run-down structure having closed to steam the previous April and had become a haven for out of use and stored diesel shunters. Hunslet 204hp 0–6–0 Diesel Mechanical Shunter No D2596 stands dead between two sister engines inside 64A. (S.Turnbull)

50) Another member of the same class carries its original number of 11167 in the yard at 30F Parkeston in January 1959. Its new number of D2564 was adopted in July 1958. No 11167 began its career based at 32A Norwich on 15th June 1957. Before condemnation in August 1967 it served from 32D Yarmouth South Town, 32B Ipswich, 30F Parkeston on the Eastern Region, with a final home at 8C Speke Junction on the London Midland Region. (N.E.Preedy)

51) Released from its birthplace of the North British Railway Company works eleven days prior to this photograph being taken on 22nd May 1960, 225hp Diesel Hydraulic 0–4–0 Shunter No D2755 stands on No 2 road outside 65A Eastfield (Glasgow) prior to making the relatively short journey to its first home at 64C Dalry Road in Edinburgh. D2755 had a lifespan of only seven years before being cut up by Argosy Salvage Co, Shettleston. (N.E.Preedy)

52) The first twenty members of this class originally carried numbers 11700–19. One example, No 11713 (D2713) proudly carries the makers plate NORTH BRITISH at the front end and the famous worksplate under the locomotive number as it stands in the yard at 62B Dundee Tay Bridge on 17th June 1958. The entire class was based in Scotland and No 11713 spent all of its working life allocated to Dundee. It was withdrawn in March 1967. (N.L.Browne)

53) The Yorkshire Engine Company also turned out a small class of 0–4–0 Diesel Shunters, Nos D2850–69, rated at 170hp. They were later classed as 02 though only four examples were renumbered as the same – 02001 (D2851), 02002 (D2852), 02003 (D2853) and 02004 (D2856). These engines were intended for use in confined spaces and some were based in Liverpool. D2857 is seen at its home depot of Allerton on 6th April 1971. (N.E.Preedy)

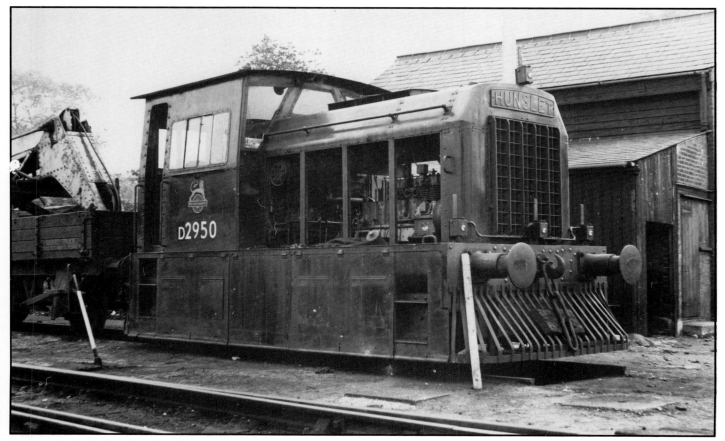

54) Hunslet built 0–4–0 153hp Diesel Mechanical Shunter No D2950 awaits attention to its engine at 32B Ipswich in the late fifties. Only three examples were constructed, Nos 11500–2, between December 1954 and January 1955, later renumbered D2950–52. In the main they were utilised on quayside workings hence the protective 'skirt' to cover the wheels. D2950 was withdrawn from normal service in December 1967 and sold to Llanelly Steel Co. (N.E.Preedy)

55) Yet another small class of 0–4–0 Diesel Shunters, four in all, were built by Andrew Barclay, Kilmarnock, numbered 11503–6. Their power rating was 153hp and were later classed as 01. They were renumbered D2953–56 between March 1959 and July 1961. In June 1974 Nos D2954/55 became Nos 01001/2. 11505 performs shunting duties at 30A Stratford in May 1956. This loco was withdrawn in March 1981 after seeing service on the Holyhead breakwater trains. (N.E. Preedy)

56) The same locomotive is also seen at Stratford shed on 8th October 1961 in its guise as D2955. Allocated to Stratford from new in February 1956 it remained there until transferred to the London Midland Region in April 1965 at 9D Newton Heath. A final transfer in June 1967 took it to 6J Holyhead. Lurking in the background is an unidentified LNER L1 Class 2–6–4T and we can just make out the bunker of BR Class 4 2–6–4T No 80131. (N.L.Browne)

57) Southampton Docks was still a busy rail-connected port when the fourteen Ruston & Hornsby 0–6–0 275hp Diesel Hydraulic Shunters Nos D2985–98 appeared in 1962, eventually replacing the SR USA 0–6–0 Tanks. Of the trio seen here on 9th July 1972 two have lost the 'D' prefix and gained the 'double arrow' logo – Nos 2987/89. The other locomotive is D2988. Each unit weighed 42 tons 5 cwt. powered by a Paxman six cylinder engine. (F.Hornby)

58) Southampton Docks shed, coded 71I and 70I, 'officially' lost its allocation of steam engines in June 1963, but continued to house them on and off until the end of steam on the Southern Region in July 1967. This fine portrait of Class 07 0–6–0 No D2996 shows it in the process of shunting stock at the depot on 19th June 1965. All members of this class were withdrawn by 1977, but a number still survive in private ownership. (N.E.Preedy)

59) The 350hp 0–6–0 Diesel Electric Shunters built between 1952–1962 became the standard large diesel shunting locomotive and were later classified in the main as 08, Nos D3000–D4192. There were a few offshoots which were classed as 09 and 10 within their ranks. On a bright and sunny 28th April 1957 No 13291 stands with a sister engine in the shed yard at 16A Nottingham. Built during 1956 it was renumbered D3291 (7/62) and 08221 (3/74). (N.E.Preedy)

60) Unlike many diesel shunters the 08's were all built by British Railways, at Darlington, Derby, Doncaster, Crewe and Horwich Works. Two of Derby's products are seen on shed at Gloucester (Horton Road) depot on 4th April 1969. On the left and in green livery is No D3994 whilst on the right No D3993 stands in newly applied standard blue livery. When first constructed different batches tended to be based 'en masse' at individual sheds. (N.E.Preedy)

61) No less than 1193 locomotives were built for BR, to the same basic 350hp diesel electric 0–6–0 shunting design. Looking the worse for wear, No D3044 is in a grubby condition, neglected by the cleaners at its home shed of 70B Feltham as it stands with a brakevan at Clapham Junction on 12th March 1967. Withdrawn in August 1974, D3044 (08032) was sold to Foster Yeoman, Merehead Stone Terminal in February 1975, becoming 33 *Mendip*. (J.M.Gascoyne)

62) No D4167 was amongst the last to be produced, built at Darlington Works and allocated to 83D Laira (Plymouth) in May 1962. When this picture was taken on 9th July 1970, D4167 was based at Newton Abbot. It is noted shunting coaching stock at Exeter St.Davids station. The loco is in blue livery with the 'double arrow' symbol stencilled on the toolbox. These versatile machines can still be seen at work from as far apart as Aberdeen and Penzance. (N.E.Preedy)

63) We move away from the world of the diesel shunters and back to the realms of larger passenger and freight hauling units and begin with the BR built D5000 series of Bo-Bo Type 2's, later classified as 24 and 25. In the transitional period between steam and diesel the two forms of traction were often paired together as are D5180 (25030) and LMS Class 4 2–6–4T No 42145 seen at Laisterdyke Junction with the 10.30am Leeds to Bradford express on 16th June 1967. (N.E.Preedy)

64) The BR Sulzer Type 2's were used in some numbers on the Highland line trains to Inverness and beyond and were often harnessed in tandem to the larger Birmingham Railway Carriage & Wagon Company built D5300 Type 2's. However, in this photograph taken at Aviemore on 18th June 1969 Nos D5119 and D5130 head south with the 16.35 hours Inverness to Glasgow and Edinburgh express which will split into two separate portions at Perth station. (N.E.Preedy)

65) Two Sulzer Type 2's at Crewe depot on 1st June 1971. Nearest the camera in blue livery, minus the 'D' prefix and sporting the modern logo is No 5056. Trailing behind 5056 and looking in dire need of an overhaul is D5064 still in green livery with the BR 'Lion on Wheel' symbol. The detail differences are quite clear on these early D5000 series of locos – no headcode panels and more air intakes on the engine side. Note the fold-over indicator discs. (N.E.Preedy)

66) Sulzer Type 2 No D5267 started its life based from 16A Toton on 2nd May 1964 and was renumbered 25117 in February 1974. Before withdrawal in January 1984 it was also allocated to 16C Derby and Cricklewood in London. On 17th May 1970 it is seen at Tramway Junction, Gloucester in two-tone green livery at the head of a rake of steel empties (6V15) bound for South Wales. It was cut up at Swindon Works during the early part of 1984. (N.E.Preedy)

67) The Class 24 Sulzer Type 2's were numbered from D5000 to D5150 and were constructed between 1958–1961. All were renumbered 24001–24150 with the exception of D5005 which was withdrawn in January 1969 following collision damage. The pioneer engine No D5000 became 24005 which under normal circumstances would have been the number allocated to D5005. On 20th June 1970 No 5148, one of the last to be built, with bodyside numbers is seen at Sheffield. (N.E.Preedy)

68) Ten years after repairs and overhauls to steam locomotives had ceased the erecting shop bays at Derby Works are filled with units of diesel traction in various states of repair. At the forefront, supported by heavy duty jacks, is Sulzer Type 2 No. 5076, noted in blue livery on 17th September 1973. Belonging to Class 24 it became No 24076 and was condemned from Crewe Diesel depot in October 1975. It was eventually cut up at Swindon. (N.E.Preedy)

69) Sulzer Type 2 No 5113, again in standard blue BR livery with the modern logo, emerges from within the dark confines of Edinburgh (Waverley) and growls its way southwards with a local stopping passenger train bound for Newcastle in the afternoon of 8th September 1971. The Sulzer Type 2's numbered some 300 units and were employed on all types of trains. All were withdrawn by/during the eighties though some are preserved in working order. (N.E.Preedy)

70) We move on to the BRC & W Type 2 Bo-Bo Diesel Electric locomotives which were built at Smethwick during 1958/59 & 1961/62. Nos D5300–D5346 (Class 26) were the earlier types, followed by Nos D5347–D5415 (Class 27). On 23rd May 1959 No D5307 passes a WD Class 8F 2–8–0 at Hatfield on a Cambridge to Kings Cross local passenger. Nos D5300–19 were based from new at 34B Hornsey for use on secondary duties on the 'Great Northern', but were drafted to Scotland in 1960. (F.Hornby)

71) Guarded by a pair of upper quadrant semaphore signals firmly set at danger, a brace of BRC & W Type 2's Nos 5410 and 5408 wait at Mallaig with West Highland line trains on 13th August 1969. These Class 27 locomotives (27059) and (27063) had a comparitively easy life before they were refurbished for high speed running on the Glasgow–Edinburgh push/pull expresses. Both had commenced their BR careers from Cricklewood shed in 1962. (N.E.Preedy)

72) Though some depots were purpose built to accommodate diesel locomotives the vast majority of sheds in the late fifties and early sixties were still devoted to the maintenance and servicing of steam engines. Therefore, depots like this one at 65J Stirling quite often had a couple of roads set on one side for the stabling and fuelling of diesels like Class 27 No D5365, seen on 10th June 1962. Note the railbus in the background. (F.Hornby)

73) The lofty and spartan tenement building situated high above Glasgow's Queen Street station had for countless years suffered pollution from the soot of steam engines. No doubt the occupants were glad to see the back of them, but after they were gone one doubts if they were too pleased with the smell of diesel fumes invading their lives from from locos like BRC & W Type 2's Nos 5397 and 5408 on duty beneath them on 9th September 1971. (N.E.Preedy)

74) Possibly the most successful type of Type 2 locomotives were the A1A–A1A Diesel Electrics built by the Brush Traction
Company in Loughborough between 1957–1962, numbered D5500–D5699 and D5800–D5862 which later became Class 31.
This fine elevated photograph shows a typical scene at Kings Cross in the late 1960's. Watched by expectant travellers on the
next platform Brush Type 2 No D5603 arrives with a semi-fast. The litter spread over the track is one of the less attractive "signs
of the times". (J.M.Gascoyne)

75) As diesel traction replaced steam at 30A Stratford (completed by September 1962) existing running sheds were demolished and replaced by new structures purely to house and look after the former. Accompanied by two sister engines, in earlier livery, No D5659 (later 31232 – February 1974), are parked at Stratford on 19th April 1969. This loco is in a high state of cleanliness as befits a Stratford machine which in the main were kept in fine condition. (N.E.Preedy)

76) Virtually in brand new condition Brush Type 2 No D5510 (30A Stratford) stands light engine in the drab surroundings of Liverpool Street station in June 1958. For many diesel enthusiasts the early livery of locomotives like D5510 (green) is far better than the dreary and ubiquitous 'standard blue' of today. D5510, renumbered 31010 in April 1974, spent all of its working life on the Eastern Region, being withdrawn in July 1976. (N.E.Preedy)

77) Brush Type 2 No 5508 at Stratford Depot in East London on 11th July 1970 having long been converted to blue livery with bodyside numerals. Stratford shed had a large allocation of these Type 2's and they could be seen on traffic of every description on the former Great Eastern lines. They also worked on passenger services to Cambridge and Kings Lynn and at times stood in for larger locomotives on the Norwich run out of Liverpool Street. (N.E.Preedy)

78) The appearance of the first Brush Type 2 diesel locomotives of the D5500 series on former Great Eastern metals in late 1957 spelled the beginning of the end for well over 100 years of steam hauled traction in East Anglia. On 19th August 1958 the crew enjoy a last minute chat before boarding No D5506 (30A Stratford) which is possibly substituting for a BR *Britannia* Class 4–6–2 with the 10.30am express to Norwich (Thorpe). (M.Joyce)

79) In direct contrast with the Great Eastern section of the Eastern Region on which Brush Type 2's took a share of 'top link' work, their Great Northern sisters mostly had to be content with less glamorous duties. No D5587, from 34G Finsbury Park, clatters over points as it passes Hitchin South signalbox on 2nd August 1960 with the 2.30pm Kings Cross to Baldock 'stopper'. D5587 later changed identities twice – 31169 and 31457. (M.Joyce)

80) Prior to the opening of Finsbury Park diesel depot in April 1960 (and afterwards) the new diesels which operated from the London end of the East Coast Main Line shared Motive Power Depots with steam locomotives. One such depot was at 34B Hornsey, north of Kings Crss terminal, where refuelling facilities were provided for the 'New Order'. In this vintage picture taken in August 1958 two Brush Type 2's are identified as D5593 and D5605. (N.E.Preedy)

81) One of the less conventional manifestations of the British Railways 'dash for dieselisation' in the late fifties was Metropolitan-Vickers 1200hp Type 2 Co-Bo design. Only twenty were built (at Trafford Park and Gorton) between 1958 and 1959, and they were destined for an active life of only ten years or less on duties like the ones from St.Pancras to Manchester. No D5710 already looks woebegone whilst visiting Crewe Works on 3rd October 1966. (T.Walton)

82) After construction the 'Metrovicks' were initially allocated to 17A Derby, but during the last years of their working lives they were exiled to the North-West, in the Barrow, Carlisle and Workington areas. The driver of No D5716 poses for the camera from the cab of his charge at Bedford station on 18th May 1959. Barely a couple of days old D5716 commands a Manchester to St.Pancras express. Although classified as Class 28 these engines were never renumbered. (F.Hornby)

83) 'Metrovick' Type 2 No D5702 has its engine idling outside the running shed at 66A Polmadie (Glasgow) on a bright, sunny August day in 1959. As can be seen by the headboard these units were employed on the short-lived *Condor*, a forerunner of today's 'Freightliner' trains, and ran from Hendon to Glasgow. D5702's short life was ended upon withdrawal in September 1968. Behind D5702 in this picture is LMS Class 4 2–6–4T No 42264. (N.E.Preedy)

84) The display of white discs on 'Metrovick' Type 2 Diesel Electric No D5712 suggests a 'Royal Train', but BR management would have hesitated to entrust such a responsibility to one of its more 'temperamental' breeds. In fact, D5712, whilst apparently receiving attention at 9C Reddish on 12th May 1968, is only one month away from retirement. The 'Metrovicks' were never a great success and many spent long periods of time in store during their lives. (Author's Collection)

85) Another of the 'less-than-successful' designs introduced by British Railways in the orgy of dieselisation of the late fifties was the Type 2 'Baby Deltic' Bo-Bo Diesel Electric, built at the Vulcan Foundry, Newton-le-Willows during 1959. All were operating on the former Great Northern line to and from Kings Cross until early withdrawal by March 1971. No D5904 is noted on a local passenger train at Welwyn Garden City during 1959. (N.E.Preedy)

86) Another photograph taken at Welwyn Garden City station, presumably on the same day. 'Baby Deltic' No D5907 is in charge of a Cambridge line express. All ten units were classified as Class 23, but like a number of the early diesels they were never renumbered and during their short lifetime only worked from two sheds, at 34B Hornsey and 34G Finsbury Park. Withdrawn in October 1968, D5907 was later cut up at Cohens, Kettering in 1969. (N.E.Preedy)

87) Having not long arrived from their birthplace at Newton-le-Willows, 'Baby Deltics' Nos D5907 and D5908 are in immaculate external condition at Hornsey as they wait to be taken officially into BR stock on 6th June 1959. The fate of D5907 has been described in the previous caption, but the ultimate end for the latter locomotive has not been ascertained fully. Condemned in March 1969 it was stored at both Hornsey and Finsbury Park depots before being scrapped at either Cashmores, Great Bridge or Cohens, Kettering. (N.L.Browne)

88) We take a final look at the 'Baby Deltics' with this photograph of No D5909, from 34G Finsbury Park, taken at Kings Cross terminus where it is in charge of a down local passenger on 26th November 1960. Like the 'Metrovicks' the 'Baby Deltics' also spent considerable amounts of time in storage whilst still in 'active' service. D5909 was the last member of the class to be withdrawn, and was cut up at Cohens, Kettering in the autumn of 1973. (F.Hornby)

89) Two of the seven main classes in the Type 2 category came from the North British Locomotive Company's stable in Glasgow, including he D6100 series of 1000hp Bo-Bo Diesel Electrics. Of the fifty-eight built, the first ten went to the Great Northern section of the Eastern Region between December 1958 and April 1959 finding a temporary home at 34B Hornsey. No D6103 is seen passing Harringay West with mail vans on 2nd June 1959. (B.W.L.Brooksbank)

90) Sister locomotive No D6104 removes empty coaching stock from within the confines of Kings Cross station on 7th August 1959. Yet another class which was destined never to carry the modern TOPS numbers, the D6100's were classified as Class 21 with some members as Class 29 when they were re-engined. By April 1960 the original batch allocated to the 'Great Northern' Nos D6100–D6109 had been drafted to Scotland, at 65A Eastfield (Glasgow). (M.Joyce)

91) Another view of D6100 series Type 2 No D6103, this time at Hornsey on 6th June 1959. It was the fate of the many Type 2 diesels stationed on the Great Northern section of the East Coast Main Line to perform on the same chores as the steam tank engines which they replaced. D6103 is hauling a rake of empty coaching stock bound for Kings Cross. Note the splendid array of upper quadrant signals on the gantry in the background. (F.Hornby)

92) D6100 series Type 2's Nos D6105 and D6108 are pictured together outside the shed at 34E New England (Peterborough) on 10th April 1960, the day before they departed for pastures new in Scotland. As already described, Nos D6100–D6109 were first stationed on the Great Northern Section of the Eastern Region. Nos D6110–D6137 went to depots on the Great Eastern section and Nos D6138–D6157 to sheds in Scotland. All were withdrawn by the end of 1971. (W.Boyden)

93) No. D6300, the first of the fifty-eight North British built Type 2 B–B's (released into traffic in January 1959) with hydraulic propulsion, gives a helping hand to GWR *Castle* Class 4–6–0 No 5028 *Llantilio Castle*, from 83D Laira (Plymouth), on Dainton Bank with an express on 22nd August 1959. All of the members of the D6300's were based on the Western Region and many worked from Laira shed on the main line and branches in Devon. (A.N.H.Glover)

94) Another 'double-header' in the sylvan setting of the South Devon countryside in high summer, sees D6300 series Type 2 (later Class 22) No D6301 helping GWR *Hall* Class 4–6–0 No 5931 *Hatherley Hall* (81A Old Oak Common) on an eastbound express, also on Dainton Bank on 22nd August 1959. Although many years the junior of *Hatherley Hall*, D6301 only outlived the former by five years or so, being condemned from Laira in December 1967. (A.N.H.Glover)

95) As can be seen in this photograph it did not take too many years for diesels to succumb to the same abysmal standards of cleanliness suffered by the majority of steam locomotives in the sixties. A group of 'grubby' D6300 series of Type 2 diesel hydraulics are stationed in the yard at St.Blazey shed in Cornwall on 19th June 1965. Nearest the camera is No D6324. Many of these locos worked west of the Tamar and often 'hunted in pairs'. (F.Hornby)

96) Brand new D6300 series Type 2 No D6343 poses proudly outside Swindon Works on 6th May 1962 after delivery from the North British Locomotive Company. Unlike earlier members of the class note that reporting number panels are recessed flush with the bodywork. Like so many of the products of the great 'Modernisation Plan', none of the class worked beyond twelve years. D6343 was taken out of traffic at Laira (Plymouth) shed in September 1968. (W.Boyden)

97) We move up a gear and onto Type 3 diesels, dealing first with the D6500 series of diesel electric Bo-Bo's of which ninety-eight were constructed (Class 33) by the Birmingham Railway Carriage and Wagon Company between 1960 and 1962. Two units, Nos 6578 and 6579 are at Exeter St. Davids on 8th August 1971 with the 14.00hrs to Waterloo. In later years they were replaced by the English Electric Type 4 D400 series of Class 50 units on this service. (N.E.Preedy)

98) All of these Type 3's were allocated to the Southern Region and based at 73C Hither Green. In this picture there are shades of the *Golden Arrow* as No D6511 wheels a Victoria bound 'Continental' through Ashford on 3rd August 1961. With the end of steam on the horizon at Ashford the third rail is in place and soon the boat trains will consist of electric multiple units. (F.Hornby)

99) BRC & W Type 3 No 6523, in blue livery, passes an express in bright sunshine at Sonning Cutting east of Reading with a train of coal empties on 23rd June 1973. These popular 1550hp locomotives have given good service and many of them are still at work today. They were renumbered 33001–33065/33101–33119/33201–33212 during 1973 and 1974 with the exceptions of Nos D6502 (withdrawn in May 1964) and D6576 (withdrawn in November 1968) after accidents. (N.E.Preedy)

100) At a time when the BRC & W Type 2's were quite a rare sight in Bristol, No D6553 in green livery, is seen coming off Bath Road Diesel Depot from a platform at Temple Meads station on 12th July 1969. In later years they were a common sight on the Western Region working Portsmouth to Cardiff services. They were also visitors to Crewe, Manchester, the North Wales Main Line and to the far south-west of Wales at Carmarthen. (N.E.Preedy)

101) English Electric had a habit of producing fine diesel locomotives and another class which came under this description were the D6700 series of Type 3 Co-Cos built at the Vulcan Foundry, Newton-le-Willows and at Darlington (Robert Stephenson & Hawthorns) between 1960–1966. No 6813 gets a heavy train of steel bars under way after a crew change at York and passes Holgate Junction on 21st March 1972. The headcode 8V85 denotes that the train is bound for the Western Region. (N.E.Preedy)

102) In contrast to the variety of designs in the Type 2 category, Type 3 was restricted to just three classes, the most numerous being the 309 members of the 1750hp D6700's. The first thirty went to the Great Eastern section of the Eastern Region at 30A Stratford, 31B March and 32A Norwich, appearing between December 1960 and June 1961. No D6723 is recorded at the Liverpool Street station buffers on 30th December 1966. (J.M.Gascoyne)

103) The first batch of these EE Type 3's to appear on the Western Region were numbers D6820 to D6958 which arrived between April 1963 and January 1965. The vast majority were drafted to diesel depots in South Wales and helped to kill off steam in the area by late 1965. Later in their lives many were transferred to other regions including the Scottish. On 17th August 1969 No D6837 is recorded at rest in the shed yard at Motherwell. (N.E.Preedy)

104) The prototype English Electric Type 3 Co-Co No D6700 first entered service on 2nd December 1960 and it is seen at its home depot of 30A Stratford on a dull and overcast 18th February 1961. These locos were designated Class 37, with D6700 becoming 37119 in February 1974. In February 1968 it was loaned to 64B Haymarket in connection with the high speed push and pull trials between Edinburgh and Glasgow and returned to 30A in April 1968. (F.Hornby)

105) Another 'first', but at a different end of the time scale. EE Type 4 No D6600 was put into service almost five years after D6700, being amongst the last to be constructed – D6600 to D6608. On 2nd February 1969 it is seen, minus 'D' prefix, still in the original green livery at Gloucester. Note the different indicator panels as compared to D6700. (N.E.Preedy)

106) With a smashed headcode panel EE Type 3 No 6774 passes beneath the magnificent roof structure at York with a transfer freight between Dringhouses and Foss Island Yards on 13th July 1971. Maids of all work, these powerful and compact diesel electric locomotives are at home on express passenger trains as well as fast fitted/unfitted goods or just plain transfer work. D6774 was renumbered 37074 in February 1974. (N.E.Preedy)

107) English Electric Type 3 No D6977 in company with a sister engine in the depot yard at Newport (Ebbw Junction) on 10th July 1968. The locomotive is in the same green livery that it was painted in when delivered new to South Wales in May 1965, along with small yellow warning panels. The heavy thud of their English Electric engines and the throaty roar at start have made these firm favourites amongst enthusiasts and many are still at work today. (N.E.Preedy)

108) The 'Hymeck' B–B Class Diesel Hydraulics built at Gorton by Beyer-Peacock during the years from 1961–1964 were all based at depots on the Western Region and became as popular with enthusiasts as the *Warship* and *Western* diesels. In common with the latter the 'Hymecks' were the only other class of diesels to carry 'proper' identification numerals. On 5th May 1971, No D7094 is seen with a freight at Netherhope Halt on the Wye Valley line. (N.E.Preedy)

109) The 'Hymecks' were another example which, although classified as Class 35, never became renumbered. In this print of No D7097, from 86A Cardiff (Canton), an attempt has been made to eradicate the 'D' prefix in order to bring its number in line with its new 'blue' image. Sporting the freight code of 8C82, No D7097 poses for the camera in the yard at Gloucester (Horton Road) on 24th July 1970, two years or so before withdrawal. (N.E.Preedy)

110) The 1700hp Maybach engine of 'Hymeck' No D7018, from 82A Bristol (Bath Road), disturbs the rural tranquility of Kemble as it pulls away from the station with its steam heating apparatus in full flow at the head of lH57, the 9.05am express from Paddington to Gloucester on 28th March 1964. Condemned from Old Oak Common in March 1975, D7018 was placed in store until July of the same year when it travelled to GWS Didcot for preservation. (F.Hornby)

111) 'Hymeck' Type 3 No D7093 comes off the Greenford line at West Ealing on 16th May 1974 with a short goods train (7A92). All in all 101 units of this 'different' diesel design were constructed. No D7093, built in late 1963, was one of the last to remain in active service, being withdrawn in November 1974 and cut up at Cohens, Kettering during 1975. (N.E.Preedy)

112) Throughout this album an attempt has been made to keep the pictures of locomotives in an approximate order of chronological numerical appearance. Therefore, with the next two prints we return to the Type 2 BR Sulzer Bo–Bo Diesel Electrics. Class 25 No 7581 (25231) heads past the shed at Polmadie (Glasgow) with a train consisting of empty coaching stock on 9th September 1971. The loco looks quite smart in its new coat of BR blue. (N.E.Preedy)

113) BR Sulzer Type 2 No D7587 first appeared on the scene at 16A Toton in March 1964 swiftly moving on to 2E Saltley in Birmingham the following month where it was based for some two years. On 22nd September 1970 it is stabled in the shed yard at Gloucester (Horton Road) still sporting its original green livery. Renumbered 25237 in November 1973 it survived in service until June 1985 and was scrapped at Doncaster Works the following May. (N.E.Preedy)

CHAPTER SIX – TYPE I DIESELS D8000–D8616.

114) The very first of BR's fleet of 'standard' diesels were the 1000hp Bo–Bo Diesel Electric Type 1's of the D8000 series introduced in June 1957. The first twenty units were based at 1D Devons Road Bow which had been converted from steam to diesel by August 1958. 'On shed' at Devons Road on 21st September 1958 is No D8005. These units were mainly used at first on transit freights around the London area over former North London Railway lines. (N.L. Browne)

115) We can just catch a glimpse of the old steam running shed behind Type 1 No D8007 at Devons Road on 13th April 1958. This section of the depot was destined to become the locomotive stabling shed as opposed to the diesel maintenance section. Eventually 229 strong these units were all English Electric powered, becoming Class 20 in the 1968 scheme. D8007 was the oldest survivor of the class in mid-1993 as No 20007 (renumbered in April 1974). (A.N.H.Glover)

116) Weighing in at 72 tons the Class 20's were yet another superb product of the 'alliance' between the Vulcan Foundry at Newton le-Willows, Robert Stephenson & Hawthorns at Darlington and Engish Electric. With its first permanent home being at 1D Devons Road Bow in October 1959, No D8037 was no stranger to the West Coast Main Line out of Euston where it is photographed 'cab first' on an empty stock train on 11th February 1961. (F.Hornby)

117) Despite becoming the first diesel depot 'proper', Devons Road shed was to close in situ on 10th February 1964 after it was ascertained that its remaining work could be carried out at 30A Stratford. Whilst still on Devon Road's books EE Type 1 No D8015 is a visitor to 1A Willesden on 15th March 1959. It moved to Stratford after the closure of Devons Road. (N.E.Preedy)

118) The later EE Class 20 Type 1's had centre headcode panels at both ends as compared with the earlier examples which sported the fold-over white discs like the ones portrayed on D8015 in the previous photograph. Nos D8184 and D8198 are seen working in tandem at Westhouses with a rake of coal empties on 19th January 1969. D8184 is in blue livery whilst its partner is still in green. They were later renumbered 20184 and 20198 respectively. (N.E.Preedy)

119) EE Class 20 Type 1 No 8116 is in immaculate external condition following a heavy overhaul and sporting the new blue livery in the late sixties at Eastfield (Glasgow). These locomotives were to be found at many depots on the London Midland, Eastern and Scottish Regions. With no facilities for train heating their main task was the movement of freight, but on summer Saturdays when heat was not required they were often pressed into passenger work. (N.E.Preedy)

120) Within months of the appearance of D8000 came the British Thomson-Houston Type 1 Bo–Bo D8200 (later Class 15) Diesel Electric locomotives rated at 800hp. All forty-four of these engines spent most of their working lives in the London area. No D8231 (in service by July 1960) is seen at 30A Stratford on 8th October 1961. The short section behind the cab houses the control equipment and auxiliaries. (N.L.Browne)

121) Although generally described as the product of B.T.H. The D8200's were constructed by a mixture of builders and electrical contractors including the Yorkshire Engine Company, one example being No D8202 pictured here at 1A Willesden on 15th March 1959. Built between November 1957 and February 1961, the D8200's were yet another class which could hardly be classed as a success and they faded from the scene in March 1971. (N.E.Preedy)

122) Another shortlived breed of locomotives were the D8400 series of Type 1 Bo-Bo Diesel Electrics of which only ten were built by the North British Railway Company during 1958. In this photograph passengers should feel privileged to be riding in Gresley coaches, so soon to give way to a fleet of new MK 1 stock, as they round a curve at Stratford on 7th June 1959. In charge of this excursion train is No D8405 from 30A Stratford. (N.L.Browne)

123) During the 1960's there was still a multitude of secondary tasks on which locomotives of modest power such as the D8400's with their 800hp engines could be employed. No D8409, seen shunting vans at Liverpool Street terminus on 30th December 1966, was one of six taken out of service in September 1968, rendering the class extinct. They were scrapped at Cohens, Kettering, Cox & Danks, North Acton and Birds, Long Marston in 1969. (J.M.Gascoyne)

124) The D8500 Type 1 Class of Bo-Bo Diesel Electrics were built by the Clayton Equipment Co. at Tutbury and at Gorton by Beyer-Peacock. Despite the involvement of two manufacturers they were commonly known as 'Claytons' amongst enthusiasts. The pioneer engine was first placed in the public eye by being exhibited at Marylebone station on 26th July 1962. No D8545 passes Motherwell shed with a train of scrap for a nearby steelworks on 7th September 1971. (N.E.Preedy)

125) The same date, but a different location. In the left of the frame a 'worker' relaxes on a makeshift 'bench' as a soon to be condemned 'Clayton' No D8586 trundles past the once busy depot at Polmadie with a train of steel tubes. Fire was a hazard with these locomotives and was responsible for the withdrawal of several of them. Although classified as Class 17 they were all withdrawn too early to be renumbered, like so many others of similar ilk. (N.E.Preedy)

126) The 117 members of the 900hp 'Claytons' were divided between the Eastern, North Eastern and Scottish Regions and created something of a record for short (if not merry) lives. Typical is No D8583, pictured at 64C Dalry Road (Edinburgh) on 12th May 1964, which just managed to see out seven summers. However, one of the 'Claytons', No D8568, passed into preservation and can be seen at the North Yorkshire Moors Railway today. (N.E.Preedy)

127) Without a shadow of doubt the most famous and popular diesels ever to work on BR (on the ECML) were the 'Deltic' Type 5 (Class 55) Co-Co Diesel Electrics, built at the Vulcan Foundry. With the distinctive arches of York station in the background No 9012 *Crepello*, introduced into revenue earning service in September 1961, its powerful Napier engines roaring, accelerates away with a Kings Cross to Aberdeen express on 13th July 1971. (N.E.Preedy)

128) English Electric 'Deltic' No 9006 *The Fife and Forfar Yeomanry* at Grantham with 1A22 Newcastle (Central) to Kings Cross express on 22nd February 1974. The locomotive is in the final livery of all-over blue, with yellow front ends. *The Fife and Forfar Yeomanry*, released into traffic in June 1961 was named at Cupar, Fife on 5th December 1964. After almost twenty years of service it was withdrawn in February 1981 and cut up at Doncaster Works. (N.E.Preedy)

129) Bright sunshine and deep shadow at Edinburgh (Waverley) on 12th May 1964. EE 'Deltic' No D9004 proudly displays the 'Thistle Emblem' as it departs with the 10.00am *Flying Scotsman* (1A35) to London's Kings Cross. D9004 was later christened *Queen's Own Highlander* at Inverness station on 23rd May 1964 and renumbered 55004 in May 1974. Twenty-two 'Deltics' were built during 1961–1962. Nos D9001–21 became 55001–21 and D9000 to 55022. (J.Wraithmell)

130) A superb portrait of EE 'Deltic' No 9019 *Royal Highland Fusilier* (named at Glasgow Central station on 11th September 1965) as it passes beneath Holgate Bridge, York on 18th July 1972 with the southbound *Flying Scotsman*. In their heyday the 'Deltics' were shared between three depots – 34G Finsbury Park, 52A Gateshead and 64B Haymarket. After they were ousted by HST's on the principal ECML trains some were drafted to York shed. (N.E.Preedy)

131) Another classic shot of a 'Deltic' at York. By coincidence the train is the *Flying Scotsman* once again, this time the northbound express. In charge of this crack train in the early sixties is No D9015 *Tulyar* (34G Finsbury Park). *Tulyar* is in green livery with a lime green lower body and white cab, a livery which suited them best. Happily, *Tulyar* is still with us in preservation and is seen regularly at many British Rail Open Days. (N.E.Preedy)

132) 'Deltic' Type 5 No 9020 *Nimbus* moves round the loco yard at Kings Cross being made ready for its next duty on 17th July 1971. *Nimbus*, together with *St.Paddy* (D9001) caused quite a stir amongst their legions of fans when they became the first members of the class to be withdrawn, in January 1980. Such were the rate of withdrawals that all twenty-two were gone within the next two years and so another legend of BR main line power passed into history. (N.E.Preedy)

133) This brief pictorial record of the 'Deltics' cannot end without reference to the prototype 'DELTIC', seen here at Doncaster wih an express – circa 1960. Built at the Vulcan Works in 1955 it ran on trials on both the East and West Coast Main Lines for several years where there was no mistaking the blue livery with white 'nose whiskers'. 'DELTIC' is preserved in the Science Museum, London. Six of the 'other' 22 'Deltics' are also preserved. (E.Light)

134) 'Too big for shunting and too slow for the main line' suggests that there was no clear function for the rather massive 650hp D9500 Class Type 1 Diesel Hydraulics. No D9500 is seen at Gloucester (Eastgate) on 4th February 1967. These were the last BR locos to be built at Swindon Works and were not seen to be successful. Built in 1964 and 1965 they were all withdrawn by BR by April 1969. Many were sold to private concerns like the N.C.B. (N.E.Preedy)

135) For a time Gloucester (Horton Road) depot was a collection point for withdrawn D9500 Class 0–6–0's (Class 14) and here we see Nos D9527, D9502, D9514 and 9518 awaiting transfer to Hull where they were stored at Dairycoates shed for a time where they awaited a final decision as to their fate. In fact all of the locos in the print were to see further service with the N.C.B. at Ashington Colliery. Today, many examples work from preservation sites. (N.E.Preedy)

CHAPTER NINE – NON STANDARD DIESEL SHUNTERS

136) In direct contrast to the locos in the previous two photographs we now move back in time to earlier diesel shunters built in the 1930's to 1950's. Five non standard 350hp 0–6–0 Diesel Shunters are lined up near to the coaling plant on an unknown sun-filled day at 21A Saltley in 1959. They are led by Nos 12067 and 12044. Some of these early variants lasted until 1972 after which a number passed into private ownership. (N.E.Preedy)

137) An interesting trio of veteran diesel shunters in a siding at Bletchley depot on 9th March 1969. Drewry 0–6–0 No D2301 (withdrawn in September 1968) is sandwiched between non standard 350hp machines Nos 12045 and 12046 (both condemned in January 1969). Nos D2301 and 12045 were later towed away for scrapping, but due to wheel damage No 12046 was cut up on site at Bletchley shed by Cohens of Kettering. The remaining 'bits' were gone by late December 1969. (N.E.Preedy)

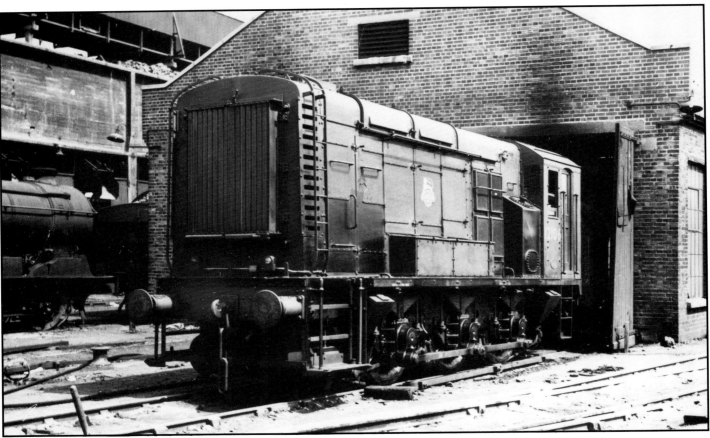

138) The non standard 350hp Class 11 Diesel Shunters Nos 12033–12138 were built at Derby Works (LMS & BR) and Darlington Works (BR) between 1945 and 1952. No 12106, constructed at the latter location in early 1952 is noted near to the monolithic coaling stage at 30A Stratford on 21st June 1953. This locomotive survived in service at Stratford until July 1970 and after a period of storage it was despatched to Booths of Rotherham for disposal. (N.E.Preedy

139) Introduced by the LNER in 1944, firstly as Class J45 and then DES 1 (1945), the four 0–6–0 locomotives constructed were closely modelled on LMS contemporaries with 350hp English Electric motors. No 15002 (originally 8002) along with the sister engines started life at Stratford shed for work at yards in East London. 15002 spent most of its life based at 31B March, though on 4th June 1967 it is seen at 5B Crewe (South) shortly before withdrawal. (P.Barber)

140) The three units of the English Electric 0–6–0 Diesel Shunters Nos 15201–15203 (SI–S3) were built by the Southern Railway at Ashford Works in 1937 and based at Norwood Junction shed. During the war years from 1941 they were seconded to the War Department, working at Martin Mill Military Railway. On 1st August 1962, a drab and dull day, No 15201 is seen at rest in the yard at 71A Eastleigh. Upon withdrawal in November 1964 it became a Departmental engine. (N.L.Browne)

141) The third member of this quaint trio, No 15203, is photographed at Norwood Junction shed on 8th March 1958. Released by the War Department during 1946 it spent some considerable time at Ashford Works before returning to its original home at Norwood. After a period of loan to the Western Region, April 1951 to July 1953, it returned (for the last time) to Norwood from whence it was condemned in ovember 1964. Cut up at Cashmores, Newport in 1966. (N.E.Preedy)

142) During 1945 technical representatives from the LMS went to the United States on a fact-finding mission following the mass dieselisation of the American Railways. As a result the first British main line diesel Co-Co English Electric No 10000 appeared in service for trials in 1947 followed by 10001 in 1948. The pair are seen in tandem at Moore with the down *Royal Scot* on 6th July 1958. Both were withdrawn in December 1963 and March 1966 respectively. (R.W.Hinton)

143) Of the early diesel prototypes 'Fell' 2–D–2 (4–8–4) Diesel Mechanical No 10100, built at Derby Works in 1950, where it is seen on 12th April 1959, must be a prime candidate for the most unsightly diesel ever built. Obtaining its nickname from one of the principal designers, No 10100 was allocated to 17A Derby in February 1952 where it was destined for a short working life, being condemned in November 1958 and cut up at Derby in 1960. (N.L.Browne)

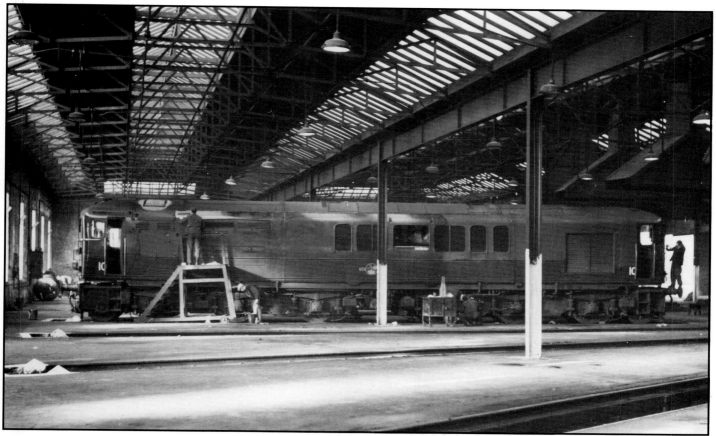

144) The Southern Region obtained its first main line diesels from within its own workshops, Nos 10201–10203 of 1Co-Co1 wheel arrangement. Nos 10201/2 appeared in 1950/51 (Ashford) and 10203 in 1954 (Brighton). On 14th December 1958 No 10203 is being attended to within the confines of the roundhouse at 1A Willesden. The loco numbers are part and parcel of the cab doors as can be seen in this photo. All three locos were withdrawn in December 1963. (N.L. Browne)

145) Another 'one-off' main line diesel was the North British Railway built (1950) Bo-Bo Diesel Electric No 10800, seen at Derby Works on 12th April 1959. After trials it was initially allocated to 1A Willesden, but after only nine short years of service it was taken out of traffic. After a period of storage at Derby Works it was sold to Brush Traction, at Loughborough, being rebuilt as a research locomotive and named *Hawk*. (N.L.Browne)

146) During 1947 the GWR ordered a gas turbine loco from the Swiss firm of Brown-Boveri. Built in 1949 it was delivered to Swindon Works in February 1950, seen here in the Works yard a decade later on 20th March 1960. Constructed as an A1A–A1A and numbered 18000 it was based at 81A Old Oak Common for use on the Paddington-Bristol line until withdrawn in December 1960. Stored at Rugby for many years it was returned to Switzerland in January 1964. (W.G.Boyden)

147) In addition to the large fleet of diesel shunters which BR eventually possessed, there were also a number of Departmental locomotives which were in BR stock. One small batch of six such engines were numbered ED2 to ED7 of 0–4–0 wheel arrangement with a 150hp engine. On 12th February 1961 No ED6, once 420045 of 1949 vintage, reposes silently in a round-house at 17A Derby, minus coupling rods. It was condemned in September 1967. (N.L.Browne)

148) 0–6–0 Diesel Shunters Nos PWM650 to PWM654 were constructed for British Railways by the firm of Ruston & Hornsby in 1952 and 1959. All were allocated to bases on the Western Region like the pioneer member of the class, No PWM650, noted in the shed yard at 82B St.Philips Marsh, Bristol on 8th May 1955. New from 1952, PWM650 was drafted into the Civil Engineers Department, Swindon in 1953 and renumbered 97650 in September 1979. (B.K.B.Green)

149) Built by English Electric in 1956, 0–6–0 Diesel Shunters Nos D226 & D227 were loaned to BR in 1957. Both were re-numbered in 1959 so as not to clash with the EE Type 4's being churned out – D0227 & D0227. These 500hp locomotives were allocated to 30A Stratford where No D227 has been cleaned and is ready for work on 7th June 1959 in its black livery with a yellow stripe. It was withdrawn from Stratford shed three months later. (N.L.Browne)

150) After operating numerous steam rail-motors earlier in the century the Great Western Railway were quick to see the advantages of diesel vehicles for economical use on lightly loaded services. A number of them were utilised on passenger workings to and from Birmingham (Snow Hill) to places like Dudley, replacing steam hauled auto-trains. No W8 built in 1936 with seventy seats, is photographed at Snow Hill in the fifties. (R.S.Carpenter)

151) These early diesel railcars were very useful on branch lines and all in all the Great Western ordered a total of thirty-eight from A.E.C., Southall which were built between 1935 and 1942. No W7, seen on a railtour at Coleford, on the Severn & Wye Joint Railway in July 1950, is, like the unit pictured above, also a seventy seater, this time built in 1935. The derelict looking station at Coleford had closed way back in 1929. (R.S.Carpenter)

152) Photographed within the diesel section of 81C Southall shed on 14th August 1960, W25 is accompanied by a diesel multiple unit. Starting life as a forty-eight seater in September 1940, W25 and a number of sister diesel railcars often worked in pairs with an ordinary carriage in between. Some were built as twin-car units with buffet facilities and others as parcels cars. W25 ended its days when it was withdrawn in August 1962. (Tim Farebrother)

153) The former GWR railcars had a distinctive growl as they gathered speed and the photographer enjoys the sounds of W20 as it leaves Great Malvern on a summer Sunday local Worcester service in 1960. W20 was one of two, the other being W19, which had dual-range gearboxes enabling the driver to select 40mph or 60mph maximum according to the duty. Condemned from 85A Worcester in October 1962 it is now preserved on the Kent & East Sussex Railway. (Tim Farebrother)

154) During the lengthy transition from steam to diesel and electric traction many older depots had to be modified to satisfy the needs of all three until purpose built sheds were built to house the latter two types. One such depot was 9A Longsight (Manchester). Peeping out of part of the 'old' shed is Bo-Bo 25kV Overhead Electric No E3041 in March 1962. Later classified as Class 84, E3041 became 84006 on 28th October 1972. (G.W.Sharpe)

155) The first section of the West Coast Main Line to be electrified with the overhead 25kV system was from Crewe to Manchester (Piccadilly) which was commissioned on 12th September 1960 after a mammoth civil engineering job on the line which lasted for three years. At Stockport station – circa 1961, is AEI (BTH) AL1 Bo-Bo Electric No E3015 with an express. These locos were in 'BR Blue' and carried a stainless steel BR emblem on the bodysides. (N.E.Preedy)

156) Prior to being rebuilt as Piccadilly, the former Manchester South Junction and Altrincham station (London Road) was closed down in September 1958 causing disruption to Mancunian rail passengers for a long time. On September 12th 1960 normal working was resumed, but with electric traction to the fore. In this photograph, again circa 1961, GEC AL4 Bo-Bo Electric No E3044 is at Piccadilly. Withdrawn in 1978 it then went into Departmental service. (N.E.Preedy)

157) In addition to being housed in the old steam shed at 9A Longsight a small electric depot was also built to ease congestion and provide proper maintenance facilties for the 'New Order'. On shed in the early sixties is GEC AL4 Bo-Bo Electric No E3036. Nos E3036–E3045 were all Class 84 and were rendered extinct in normal service by November 1980. E3036 (84001) withdrawn in January 1979 survives today in the National Railway Museum, York. (N.E.Preedy)

158) After the electrification of the Crewe to Manchester and Crewe to Liverpool routes the tentacles slowly spread between Crewe to Euston (WCML) and to Birmingham via Stafford and Wolverhampton which ultimately led to the demise of the former GWR station at Snow Hill. In its place came the monolithic concrete structure we know today. On 5th April 1969 BR/Vulcan Foundry AL6 Bo-Bo Electric No E3179 waits with a Euston bound service. (N.E.Preedy)

159) On the Southern Region the third rail system had been in being for many a year, mostly for the use of suburban EMU'S. On the 24th December 1958 the first of twenty-four units of 2500hp main line electric locomotives, Nos E5000–E5023, for use on the Kent Coast were delivered from Doncaster Works to Durnsford Road depot. No E5008 (later 71008) was new in Juy 1959 and is seen in green livery at Hither Green station in 1962. (N.E.Preedy)

160) Half-buried by the clutter of Eastleigh Works erecting shop on 11th August 1960, we find a contrast between ancient and modern, with Bo-Bo 750 volts pioneer electric No E5000 next to Adams T3 Class 4–4–0 No 563 of 1893. Later renumbered to E5024 (December 1962), E5000 was temporarily taken out of service in October 1966 for conversion to an Electro Diesel, E6104. Condemned finally in December 1977 it was cut up at Birds, Long Marston. (P.Cane)

161) Released from Doncaster Works in July 1960 and allocated to 73A Stewarts Lane, 2500hp Class 71 third rail electric Bo-Bo No E5021 finds itself in the company of a shabby Class 08 0–6–0 Diesel Shunter alongside the running shed at 71A Eastleigh on 12th March 1961. Like several sister engines it was briefly taken out of service (May 1967) and after a major rebuild at Crewe Works emerged as Class 74 Electro Diesel No E6110 (74010). (F.Hornby)

162) We take a final look at a member of the E5000 Class with this portrait of No E5018 fresh from outshopping from Doncaster Works after delivery to Eastleigh Works where it is photographed on 14th May 1960. This locomotive was renumbered to E5003 (December 1968) to fill a gap after the original E5003 was rebuilt as E6107. In December 1973 E5018 (E5003) then became 71003 until withdrawal from Chart Leacon shed in November 1977. (N.E.Preedy)

163) Still a familiar sight on the Southern Region as Class 73, the forty-nine electro diesels Nos E6001–49 were products of Eastleigh Works and the Vulcan Works at Newton-le-Willows from 1962 to 1967. Their output of 1600hp on the third rail is reduced to 600hp from an English Electric motor when running as diesels. No E6038 (73131 in January 1974) is seen with a sister locomotive in the shed yard at 73C Hither Green in April 1967. (M.P.Smith)

164) The photographer informs us that a thirty second exposure produced this effective night shot of 73 Class Bo-Bo Electro Diesel No E6048, seen halted at colour light signals at Waterloo terminus on 17th March 1967 shortly before the end of steam on the Southern. E6048 was outshopped in December 1966 and renumbered in February 1974 to 73141. One example, No E6027 was withdrawn in July 1972 following a severe accident at Horsham in January of the same year. (J.M.Gascoyne)

165) The E5000 and E6000 series of locomotives came about after the experiences learnt from the early Southern Co-Co Electrics Nos 20001–3, which proved that more powerful units were required to maintain strict timekeeping in areas with extensive multiple unit workings. BR/EE 1600hp, 750 volt D.C. Bo-Bo Electro Diesel No E6016 is way off Southern metals at Crewe Works following an overhaul on 18th May 1969. It later became 73110. (N.E.Preedy)

166) Sister locomotive No E6005 in green livery is photographed at its home base of Stewarts Lane shed on 29th September 1962, two months after construction at Eastleigh Works. In February 1974 it changed identity to No 73005. Being able to switch from electric to diesel power on non-energised sections made these locomotives very versatile indeed. Names carried by these engines include *Brighton Evening Argus* and *City of Winchester*. (N.E.Preedy)

167) We turn our attentions to the original Southern main line electrics (Class 70), Nos 20001–3, which were built at Ashford Works. No 20002 was the second of the Southern Railway's Co-Co Electric locos and originally numbered CC2 when built in 1945. It was equally at home on Newhaven boat trains or on heavy freights. This picture, at Eastleigh Works in April 1966, shows how closely the cab fronts resemble those of electric multiple units. (F.Hornby)

168) The pioneer Southern Railway 1470hp Co-Co Electric 750 dc locomotive No 20001 in ex.works condition outside Ashford Works in the early sixties. Built as CC1 in July 1941 it became 20001 in December 1948. After initial trials it was allocated to Brighton shed and it served later from Durnsford Road and Stewarts Lane. After condemnation in January 1969 it was dumped unceremoniously at Cashmores, Newport and cut up during August 1969. (N.E.Preedy)

169) Possibly the most famous of the earlier electrics were the Class EM1 Bo-Bo 1500v overhead locos Nos 26000–57, which, with the exception of 26000, were built for BR at Gorton Works. No 26000 was built by the LNER in 1941 and loaned to the Netherlands Railways from September 1947 to March 1952 and was named *Tommy* in honour of the British Forces. It started life as 6701, then 6000 and finally 26000. It is seen at Dukinfield on 1st March 1953. (N.E. Preedy)

170) Class EM1 Bo-Bo Overhead Electric No 26005 outside its birthplace at Gorton, Manchester in the late fifties in black livery. Commencing its career from Gorton shed in January 1951, No 26005 served from a variety of depots including Ilford Electric, Wath Electric and Reddish. Although most members of the class were renumbered 76 No 26005 was not included as it was condemned in March 1970 and cut up by August 1971. (N.E.Preedy)

171) The fifty-eight Bo-Bo Electric Locomotives of Class EM1 spent most of their long working lives slogging across the Pennines from Manchester to Sheffield with heavy freights, so express passenger duty may have been a pleasant change for No E26044, seen at Manchester (Piccadilly) on 27th July 1968. Redundancy for these locomotives came when electric traction ceased on the Pennine route in July 1981 . E26044 was withdrawn the same month. (J.M.Gascoyne)

172) Although erected at Gorton these electric locomotives were frequent visitors for overhaul at Crewe Works in their later years. No 26057 *Ulysses*, recorded in the Works yard at Crewe on 3rd October 1966, was the last member of the class and one of twelve which carried classic Greek names. All were named without ceremony at Gorton Works between 1959 and 1961. 26057 became 76057 in July 1972 and was condemned in February 1977 from Reddish depot. (T.Walton)

CHAPTER THIRTEEN – CONDEMNED DIESELS

173) Like the countless legions of steam locomotives which were despatched to the scrapyards by the advent of mass dieselisation in the early sixties, the same fate soon overtook some of the earlier diesel classes during the seventies. This is a sad and depressing sight at Laira (Plymouth) on 15th September 1973 where a long line of 'Western' Class 52's Nos 1020/32/42/39/38/04 and 1017 await transfer to Swindon Works for cutting up. (N.E.Preedy)

174) A similar scene of despondency at St.Philips Marsh, Bristol on 3rd November 1971 which was used as a dumping ground for redundant diesel hydraulic power prior to being despatched to suffer the same fate. From left to right are:– D815 *Druid*, D6322, D6323, D6315, D868 *Zephyr*, D819 *Goliath*, D822 *Hercules*, D808 *Centaur*, D843 *Sharpshooter*, D833 *Panther*, D855 *Triumph* and D857 *Undaunted*. To the photographer it was a terrible sight, but it had to be filmed. (N.E.Preedy)